Styles of Writing for Research Papers in Public Administration

Styles of Writing for Research Papers in Public Administration

Renae Wright-Davidson

To order additional copies of this book, contact:
Xlibris Corporation
1-888-795-4274
www.Xlibris.com
Orders@Xlibris.com
105490

CONTENTS

THIS IS DEDICATED TO THE ONES I LOVE

THE SIERRA CLUB

RENAE WRIGHT-DAVIDSON
THE ENVIRONMENTAL POLICY PARADOX,
fifth edition, ZACHARY SMITH
INSTRUCTOR: JOSHUA OZYMY
11/28/2010

The Sierra Club is the oldest and the largest grassroots environmental organization in the United States. It was founded in May 28, 1892 in san Francisco, California by the well known conservationist and Preservationist, John Muir, who became its first president. The Sierra Club has hundreds of members in chapters located throughout the U.S. and is affliated with Sierra Club Canada.

There mission is to explore enjoy, and protect and protect the wildlife places of the earth; to practice and

promote the responsible use of the earth's ecosystems and resources; to educate and enlist humanity to protect and restore the quality of natural and human environment, and to use all lawful means to carry out these objectives.

As, a member, you'll have opportunities to get involved with local chapters, as well as being part of the largest national network of environmental advocates. To become a member of the Sierra club it takes about $15.00. They are mainly supported by citizens based advocacy and lobbying efforts, contributions, gifts, donations, and dues.

Most of the members of the sierra Club in the 1930's were middle age Republicans, then later on the passage of new laws they became conservationists democrats. The members were mostly on the West Coast due to the Forestry.

During the early years they were volunteers and 500 paid staff members lobbying in Washington, D.C. They helped establish the Glacier and Mount Rainier National Parks, they helped save California Redwood Coastal Area, second National Park after Yellow Stone. They are

also responsible for implementing highways and parks all over.

The Sierra Club's most published ccrusade of the 1960's was the effort to stop the Bureau of Reclamation from building two dams that would flood potions of the Grand Canyon. They are also responsible for establishing the Redwood National Park 1970's Club, preserving Alaskan lands and eastern wilderness, and supporting Toxic Substance, Control Act of 1976, The Clean Act Amendments, Mining Control, the Surface Reclamation Act of 1977, Zero-Cut nest policy on public lands. They are activism or clean air, wetlands production, and clean energy.

There current issues today are, Land Management, nuclear issues and coal mining. For example, in land management forceful in advocating for the national forest; nuclear issues opposing building new nuclear reactors, and the less emmissions of the nation carbon dioxide due to coal. There main issues are renewable energy, restructuring energy markets, innovation, green jobs, and efficient energy use.

In conclusion, the Sierra club has a advantage over public-policy making because there is ideological bias towards increased energy consumption. Also, elected official in Washington, D.C. has a better advantage because they are private-economic interest groups always win out in environmental battles with public, non economic intest groups. In public policy-making they start with an advantage.

In summary, the resources most useful for influencing the implementation stages of the policy-making process are the traditional resources of money, political support, and information and expertise that are useful for promoting interaction with bureaucrats. Additionally, these resources musy be adequate and channeled in such away that groups can stay involved in the implementation process for the long haul.

REFERENCES:

The Environmental Policy Paradox, fifth edition, Zarachary Smith www. Sierra Club.com

ASSESSMENT OF INDUSTRY ANALYSES AND LIFE PLANNING

RENAE WRIGHT-DAVISON

MANAGEMENT 330

BENJANETTE MATTHEWS

10/30/2010

I feel all industries are effected in the following areas; globalization, technology and workforce due to the economy. These are the set of forces and conditions that originate with suppliers, distributors, customers, and competitors and affect an organization's ability to obtain inputs and outputs and dispose of outputs on a daily basis, this is called a task environment. The way a manager plans, organize, lead and control of human and other resources to achieve organization goals. Will

determine the future of how well government and private industry will function effective and efficiently.

In recent years, a great deal of attention has been focused on a new and innovative ways on quality management and techniques involved with new trends. During globalization bench marking has become a popular technique, comparing performance on specific dimensions with performance of high performance organizations.

1. In summary organizational control and change are closely linked because organizations operate in environments that are constantly changing and so managers must be alert to the need to change their strategies and structure. High performing organizations are those whose managers are attuned to the need to continually modify the way they operate and that adopt techniques like empower work groups and teams bench marking and global competitive outsourcing to remain in a global world. For example, the state government computer industry compared to Apple Computer,

for instance, we stopped saying computer and start saying Information Systems;(a system for acquiring organizing, storing manipulating and transmitting information) this information ability helps managers to make effective decisions rest on there ability to acquire and process information.

For example in my department Public sales with the sate of California, the cashiering department is used to control the amount of money taken in on a daily basis. Also the use of operating system software, application software helps coordinate and control the activities of their organization. The future is in keeping up with all new technology.

THE BUDGET DEFICIT

STUDENTNAME: RENAE WRIGHT-DAVIDSON

NAME: ECO203 PRINCIPLE OF

MACROECONOMICS

INSTRUCTOR: JEANNINE CATALDI

DATE: 06/14/2011

Ecnomists generally agree that high deficits today will reduce the growth rate of the economy in the future, why? Because it will cause unemployment rate to the ratio of the number of unemployed people to the number of people in the work force. To be considered unemployed and in the labor, a person must be looking for work. Big differences in rate of unemployment exist across demographic groups, regions, and industries. African Americans, for example, experience much higher unemployment rates

then whites. A person who decides to stop looking for work is considered to have dropped out of the labor force and is no longer classified as unemployed. People who stop looking because they are discouraged about finding a job are sometimes called discouraged workers.

Some unemployment is inevitable because new workers are continually entering the labor force, because industries and firms are continuously expanding and contracting and because people switch jobs, there is a contant process of job search as workers and firms try to match the best people to the available jobs. This unemployment is both natural and beneficial for the economy. The unemployment that occurs because of short-run jobs/skills matching problems is called frictional unemployment. The unemployment that occurs because of long-run structural changes in the economy is called structural unemployment. The natural rate unemployment is the sum of the frictional rate an the structural rate. The increase is unemployment that occurs during recessions and depressions is called cyclical unemployment.

It does matter whether the deficit is caused by lower taxes, increased defense spending, more job-training

programs,etc. Because the government influences household behavior mainly through income tax rates and transfer payments. When the government raises income tax rates, after tax real wages decrease, lowering consumption. When the government lowers income tax rates, after tax real wages increase, raising consumption. A change in income tax rate also affects labor supply. If the substitution effect dominates, as we are generally assuming, an increase in income tax rates, which lower after tax wages, will lower labor supply. A decrease in income tax rates will increase labor supply.

Also, increased defense spending should be decreased. If there is more job training then less money in the deficit. For example, the monetary policy is the behavior of the federal Reserve concerning the nation's money supply. The tools used by the federal Reserve to control the quanity of money, which in turn affects interest rate. Also, the fiscal policy government policies concerning taxes and spending. The results are discretionary fiscal changes in taxes or spending that are the result of deliberate changes in government policy.

(2) The Federal Budget deficit cannot raise its revenue in proportion to its expence, it ought, at least, accommodate its expence its revenue(Smith,1776)1976:946). There was also a quote by (Keynes,1936:129). Pyramid building, earthquakes even wars may serve to increase wealth, if the education of our states men on the principles of the classical economics stands in the way of anything better(Keynes,1936:129)

Emphasizing that institutions matter, public choice analyses of fiscal choices have shown that consitutional limits on taxing and spending can effectively constain deficit fiance and the growth of government (Porterba,1997). Certain policy of public budgetary processes and procedures have like wise been found to be significant in maintaing fiscal discipline.

(3) The late president quote Barry Goldwater "It is my earnest hope that the president and my colleagues in the Congress will give serious and penetrating through to this question. We may not any of us,

be here to witness the ultimate consequences of a continiation of this trend, but history, would be forgot that is was a challenge forfeited.

He also suggest, therefore, that by reducing high budget budget, we can begin the long much to the restoration of that right and every other privilege of American citizenship which has been submerged beneath these outrageous. For example, federal spending programs such as defense program's, job training and etc. I read one interesting article on the overall future of economics in Special Reports World Economics. "The economy and the Bible's promise A Christain Science perspective; An emerging middle clas; in countries where there essentiatially was none, has meant progress. What can bring lasting progress? A move to the middle class is a move from a life of barely existing. For example, third world continents such as Brazil, India, and China were barely earning enough money for food and housing to a new level of having discretionary income beyond these basic necessities. Those who constitute the emerging middle class become consumers and hence an engine for

economic growth. Literacy grows and educational levels expand. They begin to have a vested interest in economic stability and political freedom. Needless, to say these shifts represent huge improvements to the human conditions. But what really causes lasting economic political, and social progress? One place to look for an answer is the Bible.

It recors several thousand years of history and provides a unique perspective on the relationship between. Humanity's growing understanding of God and the resulting beneficial impact on human conditions. In other words, the economic future of human conditions has improved since the beginning of time. The global standard of living can share gratitude for God, And the article states that it is available for everyone of us to gain dominion ever all limitations of the human condition.

In conclusion the budget deficit affect overall long-term economic growth because it controld the money supply by interest rate and other sources such as (1)changing the required reserve rtio(2) changing the discount rate(the interest rate member banks pay when they borrow from the FED, and (3) engaging in open market operations(the

buying and selling of already-existing government securities. Without these factors the federal Reserve Bank couldn't increase the money supply in the United stated. It also effects our economy in the long-run such as unemployment without employment families couldn't utilize and maintain their household goods and services. The employment rate is the future for the economy and overall moral of the country, it would also help preserve basic institutions suchas schools, hospital and etc.

REFERENCES:

(1) CASE, FAIR, OSTER Principles of Macroeconomics, ninth edition, Karl E. Case, Ray C. Fair, Sharon M. Oster copyright (2007, 2009)

(2) Ashford University Library http://www.credore reference.com/entry/sprpubchoice/budget-deficits

(3) Ashford University Library articles Goldwater, Barry (morris)

(4) Ashford University Special Reports world economics The economy and the Bible's Promise,

Effective Leadership in Entrepreneurial

COURSE: MANAGEMENT 380
INSTRUCTOR'S NAME: MONICA BESS
07/20/2011

I think the effective manager for me is the entrepreneurial manager in different situations. An entrepreneurial manager needs relevant technical expertise as an invention product designer, promotter, financier or marketing specialist.

My values beliefs, self-concepts, personality and culture is best suited for Indirect Leadership has been used to describe how a chief executive can influence people who do not interact directly. "Cascading" from the CEO on immediate subordinates is transmitted down the authority hierarchy of an organization. Also, Indirect

Leadership influence the attitudes skills, behavior and performance of employees. My Trait approach emphasizes attributes of a leader such as personality, motives, values, and skills, extraordinary.

Abililities, tireless energy, penetrating intuition, uncanny foresight, and irresistible persuasive powers. I would also use the Situational Theory ("leadership substitues") identifies that conditions that can make hierarchical leadership redundant and unnecessary.

The leaders traits and influence leadership behavior. The leader skills are related to the leaders behavior on decision making. How the leader manages his time are influenced by role expectations and constraints. Self-managed techniques is why self-managed teams are successful.

What's best for me also is Center for Creative Leadership (CCL) that research on another theory. That successful top executives use the derailment Theory strong technical skills, prior success as managers "fast riser". However, the Derailment Theory has has a weak-interpersonal skills and successful to adapt to a change, build and lead a team, that's successful for me

because. I'm a autocratic leader. Vroom and Yetton calls it the ('Sell Style") rational persuasion the difference, between consulting with individuals and consulting with a group make a difference between successful and unsuccessful.

I believe strong leadership has self-confidence, strong convictions, and a passion for change. Self-Management is a set of stategies a person uses to influence and improve his or her own behavior. This would include self criticism, self-punishment, self-monitoring, self-goal setting, self-rehearsal and lt and the results would be strong self leadership.

Organizational culture is usually defined as the shared values and beliefs of members. Cultural values can enhance the performance of an organization if, they are consistent with types of processes needed to accomplish the mission and adapt to internal and external challenges. For example, shared values, such as flexibility, creativity, and entrepreneurial initiative can facilitate innovation and organizational learning. Shared values can increase efficiency.

Also, most leaders say helping each other and gender culture was difficult to deal with. Most leaders agree females are different, I agree there is a difference in leadership between male and females. Sometimes females seem to be more compationate than males and less sympathetic. It depends on the organization and vision.

Leadership behavior is influenced by other situational variables besides national culture (Bass,1990:House et al.,1997,2004). Some examples include the type of organization (e.g.,profit vs. nonprofit, public corporation vs. private ownership) type of industry (e.g. retailing, financial services, manufacturing, telecommunications, etc.) and characteristics of the managerial position (e.g., level and and function of the manager, position power, and authority). Strong values in the organization culture values, especially if an organization is a subsidiary of a foreign-owned company. The different determinants of leader behavior are not always congruent with each other. Some situational may have parallel effects across national cultures, but other situational variables may interact with national culture in complex ways.

One entrepreneurial management example was "English financier, entrepreneur, and stock market investor. Slater was chairman of the financial conglomerate Slater Walker Securities, which collapsed when the Bank of England raised short-term interest rates to slow down the economy in 1973. Property and stock markets plummeted, wiping out a substantial portion of the value of Slater Walker was eventually acquired by the Bank of England. Slater then describe himself as a minus millionare, but rebuilt his fortune and reputation, becoming a financial columnist and stock picker for the private investor (perhaps best known rates shares) and wrote as number of best-selling personal finance books.

Another example, of cultural enterprenerialship Vittorini Elio (1908-1966) novelist, essayist, translator, critic, and editor. Vittorini's importance as a novelist and essayist is equaled by his roles as a cultural enterpreneur. He was among the group, who introduced American authors, helping to air the stuffy prewar Italian literary scene. He founded and directed two of the most controversial and important post war Italian periodicalL11 Politecnice(1945-47) and 11 Menalio (2959-67). The

first, an "enlightment" attempt to create a meeting place for both Sino-Soviet and western culture after twenty years of fascist censorship, was also to serve as a point of encounter for workers and intelletuals. The avant-garde 11 Menabo focused on the literary problems of effective innovation in style and language. Vittorini also directed Einaudi's series 1 Gettoni (Telephone Token) founded in 1951 to publish translation and innovative work by young authors like Calvino. In 1964 and 1965, he founded Mondadori's Nuoviscrittori Straniere New Foreign Writers) and Einaudi's Nuovo Politecnico series. They were to introduce the lastest international trends to the Italian public and published even thing from Myrdal's Report from Chinese Village to Barthes's Elements of Semiology. By Vittorini taking advantage of his country's culture at the time he was able to be successful.

A entrepreneurial manager can take advantage of his culture or ones values beliefs and vision to produce effective manager. Using situational variable and task commitment in different types of organizations. He helps move internal and external- contraints, such as policies, rules, standard procedures, budgetary requirements, and

labor laws. Inspiring a future and vision appealed to the organization and global outsouring. This will help my enterprising as regards to globalizations.

REFERENCES:

Leadership in Organization 7th edition, Gary Yuki(2008)

Slater, Jim(1929)-(2010)-In The Hutchinson Unabridged with Atlas and weather guide htt:ww.credo reference. com/entry/helicon he/slater_jm_1929

Viitorni, Elio (1908-1966).(1996). In Dictionary of Italian Literature htt"//ww.credoreterence.com/entry/ qwitalian/vittorinia_elio_1908_1966

A SOUTH AFRICAN INVESTMENT

NAME: RENAE WRIGHT-DAVIDSON
COURSE: PHI 445 PERSONAL AND
ORGANIZATIONAL ETHICS
INSTRUCTOR: ANDREA BARCLAY

The debate over whether Caltex should continue to operate in South Africa was a moral debate. South Africa's debate was appealed to four kinds of moral standards: utilitarian, rights, justice and caring. It involved the moral character of people involved in the issues of human rights. The Judgments about justice based on moral principles, that identify fair ways of distributing benefits and burden among the members of their society. The South African

Debate is a utilitarian debate because it's a social cost effective increase debate and human right debate.

The debate over whether Caltex should continue to operate in South Africa was a moral debate. The main problems with multinational corporations like Caltex are human rights. The white South African government was committed to denying blacks their basic right, and the continued presence of American companies supported this system of brutal white rule, by African can't vote cannot collectively bargain, must live in racially segregated areas, are paid grossly discriminatory wages, are assigned 13 percent of the work force.

It is undeniable that the presence of foreign corporations in South Africa had helped to improve the real earning of blacks industrial and other workers. The income in 1970-1975 in Johannesberg, South Africa rose 118 percent, while 1980 black per capita income was only suppose to rise 30 percent. If the flow of foreign investments came to halt, the South African normal yearly growth rate of percent would drop about 3 percent over. The results would undoubtly hit the blacks the hardest, unemployment would rise (American companies employ

60,000 blacks), and whatever benefits blacks had gained would be lost. There's no doubt that the continuing operations of Caltex provided some economic support for South Africa at the end.

I believe the modification of existing South African Laws on working conditions would improve condition in South Africa. The Texaco continuation of Caltex's operations in South Africa is in the best interest of all races in South Africa.

I were a stockholder, I would vote affirmative on all resolutions because some of the laws that was voted on in May, 1983 shareholder's meetings were against the law. For example, stated "It would be a crime under South Africa's Law were Caltex-South Africa to undertake a commitment to not supply petroleum products for use by the South African military or any other Branch of the South Africa bishop Tutu, General Secretary of South African Council of Churches, would make a positive contribution to improving economic and social opportunities "I would vote affirmative on Tutu's Principles. I did also agree on the termination on companies to put pressures on the oil companies to imply with regulations.

The managers of Texaco and SoCal should have responded affirmatively and they did by giving them a request to the Board of Directors stating. If the South African Government does not within 24 months take steps to rescind the Group area Act and the influx control laws as steps toward the dismantling of Apartheid, begin the process of withdrawal from South Africa.

I do believe if a stockholder makes a contract it is there duty to and responsibility to make a high return. I feel that companies should look to law on it investments because if you don't it it just making its work for nothing because rights are derive from the legal systems and jurisdiction.

In conclusion, I feel that individual has rights as in South Africa were the blacks rights were taken away and freedom of choice was oppressed there will be civil unrest as it was in South Africa. Everyone needs to satisfy basic needs such as life, love, freedom, equality health to survive. The oil companies used the Utilitarian Principle an action is right from an ethical point of view if and if the sum total of utilities produced by that of utilities produced by that act is greater than the sum of utilities produced by any act the agent could have performed

in it's place-most utility for all is right. They are also using the cost-benefit analysis a type of analysis used to determine the desirability of investing in a project by figuring whether it's present and future economic benefits outweighs the future economic costs. Therefore, That theory might have worked in South Africa if human rights, justice and health was violated.

REFERENCES:

Velasquez,M(2006) Business Ethics Concepts and Cases (6thed.)

Jack Magarrell," U.S. Adopts Stand on Apartheid: Backed on many campuses, "The Chronicle of Higher Education,12 March 1979,

Final week-5 Business Ethics

STUDENT NAME: RENAE WRIGHT-DAVIDSON

COURSE NAME: PHI 445 PERSONAL &

ORGANIZATIONAL ETHICS

NAME OF PAPER: REFLECTIVE PAPER:

BUSINESS ETHICS

INSTRUCTOR'S NAME: ANDREA BARCLAY

11/08/2011

The debates over equality, diversity, and discrimination have been prolonged and acrimonious controversy continues to swirl around the nature of the plight of racial minorities, the equality of women and minorities and the harm they receive economically. The continuing debates over racial and sexual diversity have often focused on business and its needs, this is inevitable. Racial and

sexual discrimination have had a long history in business, and diversity now promises to have significant benefits for the future, by correcting reparity. Perhaps more than any other contemporary social issues, public discussions of discrimination and diversity have clearly approached the subject on ethical terms. The words justice, equality, racism, rights and discrimination inevitably find their way into the debate. However, there are arguments against discrimination including the utility, right, justice argument against discrimination including utility discrimination leads to inefficient use to human resources, right: discrimination violates basic human rights, Justice: discrimination results in unjust distributions of benefits and burdens. For example, some argue "Why should I pay for resparity, I didn't start slavery". However, past discrimination, in my opinion should be a social responsibility.

Title VII of the Civil Rights Act of 1964 (Amended in 1972 and 1991) for example, seems to have had this notion of discrimination in mind when it stated: It shall be an unlawful employment practice for an employer (1) to fail or refuse to hire or to discharge any individual, or

otherwise discriminate against any individual with respect to his compensation, terms, conditions, or privileges of employment because of such individual's race, color, religion, sex, or national origin; or (2) to limit, segregate, or classify his employees or applicants for employment in any way that would deprive or tend to deprive any individual of employment opportunities or otherwise adversely affect his status as an employee because of such individual's race, color, sex, or national origin. Thus these laws came into effect: Civil Right Act of 1964: made it illegal to make hiring, firing, or compensation decisions on the basis of race color, religion, sex, or national origin, Executive Order 11246: required companies doing business with the federal government to take steps to redress racial imbalance workforce. Equal employment Opportunity Act 1972: gave EEOC increased power to combat "under utilization" and to require Affirmative Action programs.

The moral philosophy and ethics in the state government are good, especially in the job I held. The government has good recruiting programs, developing and promoting women and minorities, if they don't they

will simply not be able to meet their staffing needs. I believe the organization (government) does a good job in training programs such as, Affirmative Action Programs, Sexual Harassment, and discrimination. For instance, the state has a special budget for upwards training of minority employees.

If something is not done about discrimination minorities and women statistics in poverty will be broaden. However, there are critics in the measurement for example: Official statistics of poverty in the United States and the United Kingdom show a rise in poverty between the 1970;s and the 1980's but skepticism has been expressed with regards to these finding. In particular, the methods employed in the measurement of poverty have been the subject of criticism. This paper re-examines three basic issues in measuring poverty: the choice of poverty line, the index of poverty and the relation between poverty and inequality. One general theme running through the paper is that there is a diversity of judgments which enter the measurement of poverty and that is necessary to recognize these explicitly in the procedure adopted. There is likely to be disagreement about the choice of

poverty line, affecting both its level and its structure. In this situation, we may only be able to make comparisons and not to measure differences, and the comparisons may lead only to a partial rather that a complete ordering. The first section of the paper discusses the stochastic dominance conditions which allow such comparisons, illustrating their application by references of data for the United states. The choice of poverty measures has been the subject of an extensive literature and a variety of measures have been proposed. In the second section of the paper a different approach is suggested, considering a class measured satisfying certain general properties and seeking conditions under which all members of the class (which includes many of those proposed) give the same ranking. Those skeptical about measures of the poverty and equality are being confounded. The third section of the paper distinguishes four different viewpoints and relates them to theories of justice and views of social welfare.(Atkinson,Jull.,1987)

Here is an example of some statistics of %

Percent of Whites, Blacks, and Hispanics Living in Poverty, 1978-2002, Alternate Year

YEAR	% WHITES IN POVERTY	% BLK IN POVERTY	% HISPANICS
2002	8	24	22
2000	7	23	22
1998	8	26	26
1996	9	28	29
1994	9	31	31
1992	10	33	30
1990	9	32	28
1988	8	31	27

YEAR	% WHITES IN POVERTY	% BLK IN POVERTY	% HISPANICS
1986	9	31	27
1984	10	34	28
1982	11	36	30
1980	9	33	26
1978	8	31	22

Source U.S. Census Bureau, Historical Poverty tables, Table 2. "Poverty Status of People by Family, Race, and Hispanic Origin 1959 to 2002", accessed August 5, 2003

htt://ww.census.gov/hhes/2.poverty/histpov/hstpov/2.html

In conclusion fundamental perspective developed here is the view that ethical behavior is the best long-term business strategy for a company and government, by this I do mean ethical behavior is never costly. Nor do I mean that ethical behavior is always punished. It is a behavior in fact, that ethical behavior always pays off, and that unethical behavior can impose serious losses on a company with long-term range strategy with competitive advantage. As, globalization process by which the economic and social systems of nations are connected together so are cultures, values, beliefs. If Americans are to compete and revitalize the economy they must be able to handle diversity and conduct ethical behaviors.

REFERENCES;

Veslasquez, M.G.(20060 business Ethics, concepts and Cases (6th ed)Pearson Prentice Hall, New Jersey

Ashford Library: On the Measurement of Poverty, A.B. Atkinson Econometrica,Vol.55,No.4 (Jul.,1987) (pp.749-764)